TULSA CITY-COUNTY LIBRARY

S0-AXK-967

bRjc
5/2019

TULSA CITY-COUNTY LIBRARY

BIRDS

of every color

by

Sneed B. Collard III
Photos by Sneed B. Collard III and Braden Collard

Copyright © 2019 Sneed B. Collard III

ALL RIGHTS RESERVED. No part of this book may be reproduced, transmitted, or stored in any information retrieval system in any form or by any means, graphic, digital, electronic, or mechanical, including photocopying, reprinting, taping, and recording, without prior written permission from the publisher or copyright holder. For information about permission to reproduce selections from this book, write to Permissions, Bucking Horse Books, P.O. Box 8507, Missoula, Montana, 59807 or email publisher@buckinghorsebooks.com.

www.buckinghorsebooks.com

Distributed by Mountain Press Publishing Company, Missoula, MT
800-234-5308
www.mountain-press.com

Names: Collard, Sneed B., author. | Collard, Braden, illustrator.
Title: Birds of every color / Sneed B. Collard III ; photos by Sneed B. Collard III and Braden Collard.
Description: Missoula, MT: Bucking Horse Books, 2019.
Summary: A first look at the variety, roles, and sources of colors in birds, featuring photographs by the author and his son.
Identifiers: LCCN 2018913423 | ISBN 978-1-7328753-0-2
Subjects: LCSH Birds--Juvenile literature. | Adaptation (Biology)--Juvenile literature. | CYAC Birds. | Adaptation (Biology). | BISAC JUVENILE NONFICTION / Animals / Birds
Classification: LCC QL676 .C65 2019 | DDC 598--dc23

Cover and book design by Kathleen Herlihy-Paoli, Inkstone Design, Missoula, MT.

The text of this book is set in Gill Sans and Optima.

Photography Credits
Braden Collard: Front Cover (cardinal, Green Jay); Title Page; pages 4, 6, 7, 18, 22, 27, 30, 31, 32 (trogon), 35
Page 2-3: mspoll-Shutterstock.com
All other photos by Sneed B. Collard III

Manufactured in the United States of America

10 9 8 7 6 5 4 3 2 1

Front Cover: Andean Cock-of-the-Rock (Peru)
Title Page: Green Jay (Texas)
Back Cover: Blue-footed Booby (Ecuador)

To Dennis and Stephen,
Love,
Sneed and Braden

Birds come feathered in every color.

The colors of birds are truly amazing, but these colors aren't to entertain us. Every bird color and pattern has a purpose and a story behind it. Many will surprise you . . .

From cardinal reds.

Male Northern Cardinals have some of the most vivid reds in the bird world. Brighter colors show that a cardinal is healthier than other males. This radical red also tells a female, "I have a great territory to raise a family in." It's no surprise that female cardinals pick the brightest males to mate with!

To bluebird blues.

The brilliant blues of a male Mountain Bluebird also send important messages. These include, "I am healthier than other, duller males," and "If you mate with me, your babies will be healthier, too." Again, females pick brighter males to mate with. In most species of birds, males are "showier" than females. Females blend in more with their surroundings. This helps protect them from hawks and other predators.

To oriole oranges.

More than thirty species of orioles, including Altamira (above) and Audubon's (right), live in North and South America. Almost all of them come feathered in orange, yellow, and black—often with a splash of white! Ornithologists—scientists who study birds—guess that an oriole's colors send messages that are similar to "cardinal reds" and "bluebird blues." What are those messages? That's the tricky part. Ornithologists have studied the colors of many birds, but they have not studied the colors of *all* birds. More scientific research is needed!

And a thousand colors in between.

To get an idea of how many bird colors exist in the world, look no further than tanagers. These spectacular birds come feathered in almost every possible color. Only a few kinds of tanagers spend time in the United States. To really appreciate these birds, travel to Central and South America. There, you will find more than two hundred tanager species—including Flame-faced and Black-capped Tanagers from the country of Ecuador.

Birds get colors from foods.

The colors of many birds come from pigments. Pigments are like little dabs of paint inside of feathers, beaks, and skin. Birds have two main kinds of pigments. Carotenoids (KEHR-uh-teh-noydz) produce the dazzling reds, yellows, and oranges of birds. Birds can only get carotenoids by eating foods that contain them—usually fruits, flowers, fungi, and leaves. This Summer Tanager is eating carotenoids right now!

And make them on their own.

The second main kind of bird pigments are melanins. Birds—and many other animals—make melanins themselves. Melanins are not as bright as carotenoids. The browns and blacks of this Long-billed Thrasher come from melanins. Melanins can also produce gray, red-brown, yellow-brown, and light yellow colors.

Some colors are built into feathers.

Not all bird colors come from pigments. Feathers are made from a substance called keratin (KEHR-uh-tin)—the same stuff as your fingernails.

When keratin is layered just right, it separates light into its different colors and reflects only certain colors back out. Scientists call this kind of color *structural coloration*. Structural coloration creates most of the blues, purples, and violets found in birds—including the shimmering blues of this Blue Jay!

Skin colors usually come from pigments, but in rare cases can be produced by structural coloration. In skin, structural colors aren't made by keratin. Instead, they are made by a substance called *collagen* (KAWL-uh-jen). Both collagen and carotenoid pigments create the famous bright blues and greens in the feet of Blue-footed Boobies. These bright feet reveal how healthy boobies are—and help other boobies decide which mates to choose.

And in this case, skin.

Bird colors shout,
"Choose me!"

The Andean Cock-of-the-rock is the national bird of Peru. Males gather together in groups called leks. They try to outdo each other with head bobbing, wing flapping, loud calls, and more than anything, their stunning colors. In fact, males try to stand in the best light to show off their orange feathers, or plumage. Females (right) stand nearby, judging these performances and deciding which males to mate with.

"This is my territory!"

Like many male birds, male Yellow-headed Blackbirds and Common Yellowthroats (right) stake out and defend territories during mating season. This helps them control the best possible nesting and feeding areas. That, in turn, helps them attract females. Birds that defend territories are often brighter and bolder than other birds. This warns other males: "If you come here, you're in for a fight!"

And "Back away. I'm top bird!"

In a flock, certain birds sit higher in the pecking order than others. The size and darkness of their markings often identify these "top birds." Black-capped Chickadees with blacker blacks and whiter whites on their faces rule their flocks. When these birds want to perch—or feed at a bird feeder—other chickadees get out of the way!

They help answer the questions, "What do you want?"

Male Red-winged Blackbirds have red-and-yellow patches on their wings. During mating season, males with bright patches often attack each other as they fight for territories and mates. However, unlike a Yellow-headed Blackbird, a male Red-winged Blackbird can cover up its colors with feathers. This tells other males, "Don't worry about me. I don't want your territory or mate. I'm just passing through."

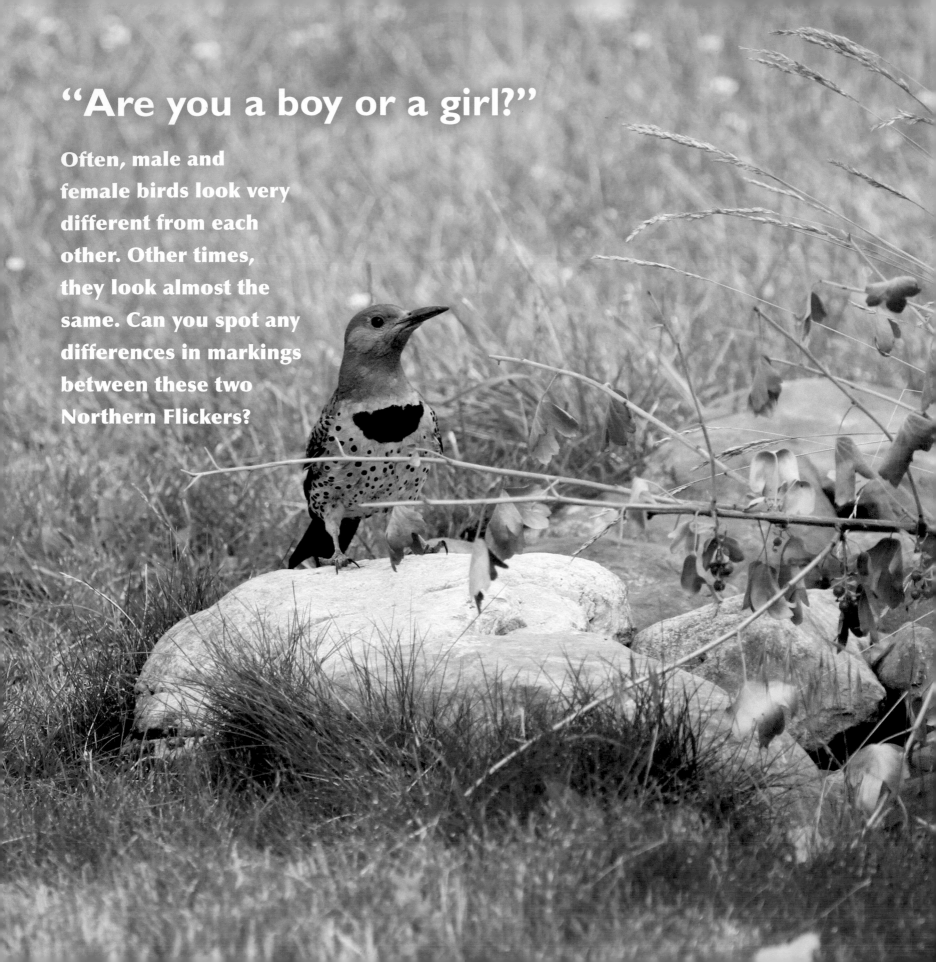

"Are you a boy or a girl?"

Often, male and female birds look very different from each other. Other times, they look almost the same. Can you spot any differences in markings between these two Northern Flickers?

That's right! The bird on this page has an orange slash on its cheek while the opposite bird does not. This marking is called a *malar patch* and shows that a flicker is a male. In one experiment, a scientist added a malar patch to a female flicker. The female's mate chased it away until the malar patch was removed!

And
"Are you mine?"

Birds use colors to recognize their own— and different—species. Birds, though, also use colors and markings to recognize *individual* birds of their own kind. Seabirds and shorebirds, such as this Western Gull, often nest in huge colonies. Fortunately, each baby seabird has slightly different colors and markings. Parents use these differences to pick out their offspring from the crowd.

Colors can go big.

It's hard to miss a male Magnificent Frigatebird when it's advertising for a mate. To attract a female, a male frigatebird builds a stick nest and then sits in it. When a female flies over, the male begins vibrating his wings and inflates his enormous red throat pouch. With a little luck, the female will be impressed by this performance and choose him for her mate.

Or barely peek out at all.

Bright colors come with a downside. They attract the attention of hungry predators. Many birds overcome this problem by having only a tiny patch of color.

With their drab gray and green feathers, male Ruby-crowned Kinglets blend in with branches and leaves. But they also have a tiny "jewel" of red on their heads. They keep this covered until they want to flash a message to a possible mate or another male. Hopefully, a predator won't notice!

They can shimmer and gleam like metal—especially if you're in the right place.

Hummingbirds such as this Velvet-Purple Coronet are famous for their shiny, metallic hues. These colors are produced by iridescence (EAR-uh-DEH-sense)— a kind of structural coloration created by the birds' feathers. With iridescence, the colors you see depend on the angle at which you are viewing the bird. More than other types of colors, iridescent colors depend on direct sunlight to really shine.

Brown colors help birds hide.

Check out this pile of sticks. Uh, wait. That's not a pile of sticks. It's a bird called a Common Pauraque (paw-RAW-kee)! Pauraques belong to a group of birds called nightjars. Nightjars have some of the best camouflage, or "blending in" colors, of any animal. Brown and gray feathers help nightjars ambush their insect prey and hide from predators. Brown colors are so useful that they are among the most common colors found in the bird world.

In a zoo, a parrot's green feathers look dazzling, but in a tropical forest, "parrot green" provides excellent camouflage. Parrots' bodies actually make their own special kinds of pigments called psittacofulvins (SIT-uh-ko-FUL-vinz). To produce the color green, yellow psittacofulvin pigments mix with blue structural colors of parrots' feathers. Just like mixing blue and yellow paint, this combination creates green.

So do many greens.

Whites, grays, and blacks? They can blend in, too.

From above, a swimming Galápagos Penguin's black back blends in with dark waters below. From underneath, its white belly blends in with bright light streaming down from the surface. Scientists refer to this "two-toned" pattern as *countershading*. Many seabirds have countershading

colors. Their black or gray colors come from melanins. Their white feathers allow *all* colors of light to pass through them. When mixed together, these colors produce white! Countershading probably helps penguins sneak up on their prey—and protect the birds from hungry predators. It may help Black Skimmers and other flying seabirds in similar ways.

Whichever colors birds come in,
one thing is certain . . .
Colors help birds survive!

Scientists still have a lot to learn about bird colors, but one thing is for sure: bird colors are no accident. Colors are important adaptations for every bird's survival. They have developed, or evolved, right along with every other bird feature to keep birds safe, help them find a mate, and allow them to succeed for generations to come. How do the colors of this Many-colored Rush-tyrant (left) or Chestnut-breasted Coronet help them survive? Scientists can make good guesses, but they don't yet know for sure. Maybe, just maybe, you'll be the person to find out!

How many bird colors do you see?

Golden Tanager

Masked Trogon

Song Sparrow

Common Redpoll

Sparkling Violetear

Bullock's Oriole

Cedar Waxwing

Lazuli Bunting

Rose-breasted Grosbeak

Great Kiskadee

Blue-and-yellow Macaw

Roseate Spoonbill

Colorful Words

camouflage—colors or other features that help an animal blend in with its surroundings

carotenoid—a kind of pigment (color) that comes from plants or fungi

collagen—a kind of protein that helps hold tissues together in an animal's body

countershading—"two-tone" coloration that camouflages an animal from both above and below

evolve—to change over time; especially when one kind of living thing changes into a new kind, or species

flock—a group of birds spending time together

iridescence—the separation of direct white light into many different colors by feathers or other structures

keratin—a major substance used to make feathers, hair, horns, fingernails and other tough structures in a body

lek—a group of male animals performing displays to attract females

mate—a partner for raising young

melanin—a kind of pigment made by living things to produce mostly browns, blacks, and grays

ornithologist—a scientist who studies birds

perch—any object that a bird sits on

pigment—substances (proteins) that produce colors in living things

plumage—feathers

predator—an animal that survives by eating other animals

psittacofulvins—a special group of pigments made by parrots

reflect—to bounce off of, as in light reflecting off of feathers

species—a particular kind of living thing

structural coloration—colors produced by the separation and reflection of light by feathers and other features in a living thing

territory—an area controlled by animals, usually to obtain food and/or raise a family

About the Author

Sneed B. Collard III graduated with Honors in biology from the University of California at Berkeley, and has written more than 80 books for young people and adults. His recent titles include *Woodpeckers: Drilling Holes and Bagging Bugs; One Iguana, Two Iguanas: A Story of Accident, Natural Selection and Evolution,* and *Hopping Ahead of Climate Change—Snowshoe Hares, Science, and Survival,* which was a finalist for the Green Earth Book Award and the AAAS/Subaru/Science Books & Films Prize for Excellence in Science Books. To write *Birds of Every Color,* Sneed spent many years observing colorful birds and reading the work of scientists. He also consulted with one of the world's top experts on the colors of birds, Professor Geoffrey E. Hill of Auburn University. To learn more about Sneed, his books, and author visits, explore his website at www.sneedbcollardiii.com and follow Sneed and Bucking Horse Books on FaceBook.

About the Photographs

The photographs in this book were taken by Sneed and his son Braden during the course of several years. They feature birds from the states of Montana, Texas, Arizona, and California as well as the countries of Peru and Ecuador. To follow Sneed's and Braden's birding adventures and photography, subscribe to their blog, www.fathersonbirding.com.